Where My River Meets The Ocean

20 Poems for 2020

Justyna Kostek

New Netherland Publishing
Schenectady NY

Copyright © 2022

ISBN: 9-780937-666746

Published by
New New Netherland Press
835 Central Parkway
Schenectady, NY 12309

Printed in the USA

Table of Contents

Dedication

I dedicate this poetry book to my beloved grandma Regina Snopczynska, the best dancer and singer I know. She was, is, and will always be my inspiration to create!

Foreword

Dear Traveller:

I am so happy to meet you along the way. Hope the words in this book will open your heart to the love that is available for us.

Wild horses and the ocean brought all the words in this book to me.
They are a symbol of the deepest freedom.

This freedom is so fragile right now.

As a way of saying *Thank You*, I am donating a percentage of the profits from the sale of this book to the Oceana Organization (Protecting The World's Oceans) and to the American Wild Horse Campaign (Fight To Defend America's Wild Horses).

Love and Peace to All,

February 2022

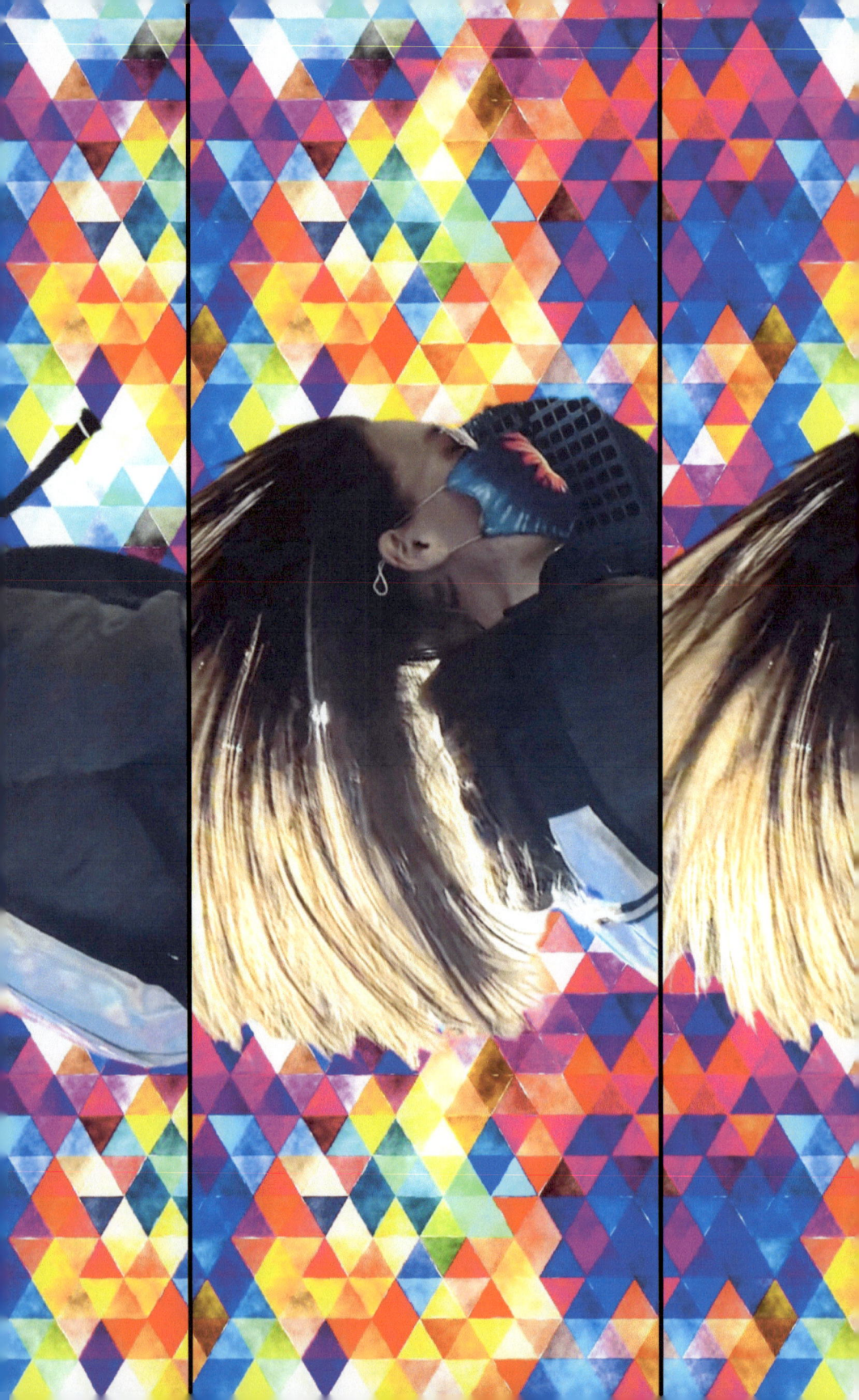

A Certain Darkness
Is Needed To See The Stars

Rainy day
"Everything happens for a reason"
You say
Sadness on my horizon
Knocks to my door
I don't want it no more
Just happiness please
And constant bliss
But it opens the window
And penetrates my soul
It leaves a cigarette burning my heart
I didn't give it a good start

A certain darkness is needed
To see the stars
A certain bravery is needed
To go to Mars
A certain light is needed to see the sky
That's why when I look at you
I say my oh my
We are gonna fly high
Oh yeah
We are gonna fly high
Just don't say why oh why
Even if you have to cry

Go with the current
Don't swim against the river
It knows it's time
To release
So you can be in constant bliss
Open the door
And dance with the darkness
As if you were the best life partners

Am I Insane To Let It Rain?

You said I don't need to strain
That's good
Because I don't want to use your cane
And while you're on it
Take away your chain
Because I think
I'd rather go insane
Than live in your brain

Am I insane?
To let it rain?
What if it doesn't drain
And I will be stuck with the rain

You should express you say
You should confess you say
All your desires
And yesterday's wild fires
I said I'd rather keep them
In my head

But then I fell in love
I couldn't keep it inside anymore
So here it is
See my whole mind's store
Opening the door

Be The King And Sing

Keep seriousness for the grave
That's the only way you might save
The flowers
And mysterious blissfulness showers
Laugh at it all
And have a constant ball
When you think you know what you saw
Look again
There is so much more

Instead of building towers
Be the king
Of the present moment
And sing
And sing
And sing
Let the dance of life begin
I promise you
It's not a sin

Run after butterflies
Walk the road with the sun
Talk to the moon
Be the first one
To greet a raccoon
Hug the tree
Treat it as if it were me

Blind Man Cannot Think About Light

He walks to the store
And forgets
What he came here for

He calls his mother
But he would like to be with you
Rather

Blind man
Cannot think about light
Deaf man
Cannot think about music
A man in love
Cannot think at all
All he does
Is speak with his soul

He walks down the street
And loses a direction
Asks everyone
What's the name of this intersection?

He lives with the feeling
Of love
And no longer needs a boxing glove
To fight with existence
He simply allows it
To be

Both Wings Are Needed to Fly

Wings of the bird
Both are opposites
And both are needed to fly

Left and right leg
Both are opposites
And both are needed to walk

Night and day
Both are opposites
And both are needed to live

Me and you
Both are opposites
Yet both can't agree

Love is not enough
You see
Love is all we've got
You see

I thought I found the key
Sitting under the tree
And thinking
How would it be
If me and you would both agree

Be my bird
Be my leg
Be my night
And don't let me out of sight

Don't Go Dying Before Death

Girl carrying the Valentine's card
To her first love
Said to me afraid
"I don't want to get hurt"
She turned around
Lost her chance
Of first romance

Grandmother walking away from her husband's
grave
Said to me afraid
"I don't think I'll ever love again"
She said "no" to the honeymoon in Spain
She'd much rather live in pain

A man meeting his son for the first time
Said to me afraid
"I don't think I can do this"
He'd rather dismiss
Than live the life's bliss

So I said to them
Don't go dying before death
The birds are singing
Don't go dying before death
The trees are ringing
Don't go dying before death
It's only your upbringing
Because
Hey you
Life needs you to be here too

MM-UNITY SPIRIT   DON'T FORGET THE LOCALS

Have The Courage To Be A Stranger

Say hello and goodbye
But don't sigh
Staying within yourself
Living from the top shelf

You are your own
Park ranger
Be the game changer
Like a power ranger

Have the courage to be a stranger
Have the courage to live in danger

No need of support
Maybe some sort
Of love
Lifting you from the above

The river flows by itself
Within you
No need to push it
Let it flow
Let it flow
Let it flow
By itself
Living from the top shelf

Hey There is Another Way

Let's talk
And go for a walk
Although you might be in shock
About what you see
Around the block
It's the life's stock

Hey there is another way
Its okay
Everything can wait
You don't have to catch the bait

The moon tonight
Brings up the light
To the site
Do you see the star's flight?
They hope that you just might
Let them write
On your heart
All the art
Of the universe
So let yourself be immersed
Because
Hey there is another way

I Can Point At The Sun
But I'm Not The Sun

I can point at the moon
But I am not the moon
I can point at the river
But I am not the river
I can point at the sun
But I am not the sun
I can show you the direction
But I can't walk with you

Walk your walk
Of life
Alone
Go into the unknown
And enjoy it
Embrace it
This is your walk
No need to talk
To anyone
Like me
You see?

I can show you the stars
But I am not the stars
I can show you the sky
But I am not the sky
I can show you the ocean
But I am not the ocean

Enjoy your silence
Worth a million
Words
Fly like a bird
And you will find
Yourself
In a middle of your journey

I won't be there
But you won't need me
I swear
For the first time
You will meet yourself
instead
And the view of the sun,
river, ocean
Is gonna spread

Is There Anyone Behind These Eyes?

Is there anyone behind these eyes?
Seeing the sunset
In all the colors
Of the rainbow

Is there anyone behind these ears?
Listening to the symphony
Of birds
Singing outside the window

Is there anyone behind these muscles?
Carrying a new born child
Home
For the first time

Is there anyone behind these lips?
Speaking the poetry of tomorrow
To my ears

I can feel your being
But I can't feel your presence
Bring your presence to me
Bring your presence
Behind these eyes
Behind these ears
Behind these muscles
Behind these lips

Let your heart meet mine
I promise you
It doesn't cost a dime

Live My Life With A Song

We go on the road
Travel together
Nature everywhere
We don't care
About the wear and tear
Everyone saluting us
We are riding our bus
To the music land
I can't wait to put my feet
In the sand

It won't be too long
Until I live my life with a song
We'll be so strong
And you'll come along
With life's new song

This is it
This is the life I want
I dreamt about it for years
If I only knew how easy it was
To find heaven's stairs
We are in tune
With the moon
And sun greets us
Every afternoon

Look Up And Mind The Gap

Look up they said
Look up
Take a map
And mind the gap

Look down they said
Look down
Since you are from another town
Otherwise you'll drown

Look left they said
Look left
There is a lot of theft

Look right they said
Look right
Or your dog will steal your bite

I go straight
Even though that's out of date
Opening the gate
To living free
You can find me
Dancing with the sea

Where no one tells me
What to do
This is where
I will wait
For you

Loud Clouds

Loud clouds
Without doubts
Do you hear them shout?

Sitting here
Not so near
To you
Dear

Loud Clouds
Without doubts
Telling you
You'll get through
And understand
Everything
Is new

Everything is new
Except for me and you

So when you look at me
There are no clouds
That I see

I leave the clouds where they belong
And I promise I won't be long
I need to listen to them shout
And find out
What
Is this all about

Love Out Of Your Own Being

I thought love depended on the other
I was wrong,
Rather.
Now I'm seeing you gotta love
Out of your own being.

Love that depends on the other
Is a poor love
Love out of your own being
Like a dove
Ocean of love surrounds you
Nothing binds you

I was so thirsty
Living on the other's mercy
Then felt so
So powerful
Like a flower
When a rain shower fell
And it gave me a chance to grow
It's unlike anything
I ever saw

Nothing Is Said But
Everything Is Understood

You're no longer here
I can't see you dear
I can't give you your favorite beer
There is nothing to steal
From your dinner plate

You're no longer tired
On the contrary
You are inspired
By the afterlife
Without your wife

Nothing is said
But everything is understood
Oh, it feels so good
To be here with you
Where you always held me tight
Despite your grumpy mood

You're no longer in my arms
Selling me your charms
And spreading your dimples
Like a dime

You're not painting
The fence
Where we used to dance
And you're not asking me for another chance

Under this tree
I will bury me
So we can be together
Forever

The Poetry Of Dance

Brings out the romance
Some say it doesn't make sense
But I know it's all in our hands

Life is a cabaret
You know
When you think you saw it all
There is always more
To dance for

Let's dance for all the mothers
They are here for you
Even if you don't see them
They always come in when you're
Feeling blue

Let's dance for all the animals
Looking at us
With their honest eyes
I always ask myself
When I look at them
How are you so wise?

Let's dance for all the unspoken words
Which we overheard
Somewhere
In the middle of silence

Let's dance for all the people
Suffering
In the world
Bring them light
So they can have a smooth flight

Let's dance for you and me
Let's dance for you and me
Please put on some tea
Cause you see
Life is a cabaret you know
When you think you saw it all
There is always more
To dance for

Things Don't Exist In The World

Things don't exist in the world
Only event
Do you feel the scent?
That's the present moment
Knocking to the door
Makes me wanna roar roar roar

Existence plays the song
I am just the gong
Vibrating its waves
The more present moment
I crave
The more lives I save

Just be it
Just be it
You don't need to see it
Believe
And then
You won't get deceived

Hear the sound of the gong
It will make you strong
And I promise
It won't be too long
Until you live your life with a song

Why Are We In Constant Motion?

Why are we in constant motion
When there is an ocean of emotion
Waiting
To reveal the waves
Underneath the sand
Of caution

Stop
Stare
Be bare
Love the place where
With you
So much
I dare

No motion
Equals emotions
And is the best
For the art
Of your heart

You're An Island

You're an island
In a middle of ocean of silence
No
There is no place
For the violence

You're one
Even though you're not done
And you're gonna see the sun
If you are not gonna
Run run run

No is your mind
And yes is your soul

No is your mind
And yes is your soul

Look at us
Winning the happiness bowl
Strolling together through any weather

Say YES YES YES
Say YES YES YES

Uno
Dos
Tres
No stress!

You Can Take My Shoes And I'll Still Walk

You can take my shoes
And I'll still walk
My feet will carry me
Wherever I'd like to be

You can take my music
And I will still sing
What's external doesn't give me wings
Every note comes from within
And you call that sin?

The love I have
For myself
Is not blind
It has eyes bigger than yours
It can see what you couldn't dream of
That's love my dear
That's love
That's love you can't get rid of

You can take the roof over my head
Cause without it
I can see the stars
And for the first time
I can hear life's guitars
Playing the chords
Of an open sky

I see you dancing under my roof
To my music
In my shoes
But I don't feel like I can lose
If you gain your joy
By taking what you think is mine
it's a good sign
I'll share
I'll share
With you
Just because I dare
Just because I dare

41

FINIS.

www.ingramcontent.com/pod-product-compliance
Lightning Source LLC
Chambersburg PA
CBHW042131080426
42735CB00001B/45